For the children, both within and before us.

May these affirmations always echo the truth: You are enough, just as you are. May you always look back with a smile and, and never carry the scars of yesterday.

With unwavering love & support,
Devin-Leigh

Colours of Confidence

Rhyming affirmations for kids

By Devin-Leigh Hunter

When I am sad and feeling blue, there is something I like to do.

It makes a big difference, and reminds me i'm strong. It is good advice. I'd like to pass it along.

I take a breath and shut my eyes tight.

I repeat affirmations, until I feel alright.

Affirmations are phrases, so simple and true.

I am loved

They help me feel better, and they can help you!

We will go through each of the colours, and smile along the way.

We will find the treasure at the end of the rainbow, and have a great day!

Don't be worried, do not fret. Affirmations are easy, you won't break a sweat!

Day or night, night or day, affirmations guide our way.

So snuggle in close, and get ready for a smile! We are going to do some affirmations, it may take a while!

Let's say them together. Are you ready? out loud! We are stronger as a team, so say these words proud!

Red is beautiful, just like me!

I find beauty in all that I see.

Red red, like fire shines bright. I am strong, with all of my might.

Confidence in all that I do, I believe in me, it's true!

Orange, orange, full of glee! I am happy, wild, and free.

Laughter dances in the air, I'm unique, beyond compare.

Yellow Is bright and kind like me!

I appreciate every part of me that I see!

Green, green, like nature's embrace. I grow and learn at my own pace.

GREEN

With curiosity I explore and find, wonderful treasures within my mind.

Green, green, I take my time.

Learning and growing, like leaves on a vine.

Blue, blue, calm and true, I'm peaceful in that all I do.

Breathing deep, worries fade. I find courage. I am unafraid.

Blue like the sky, and blue like sea.

I do my best, and stay true to me.

Indigo is a lovely colour, too!

It's unique, just like me and you.

Indigo, indigo, blueberries and blue flowers.

Creativity in my hands, like my own superpowers!

Violet and purple go hand-in-hand with glee.

They are both lovely, just like me!

Purple, violet, a lavender place. I am loved, and full of grace.

Believing in me is what I do. I believe in me and I believe in you, too!

Remember these words, every second of every day. Repeat them to yourself, so they never go away.

The treasure at the end of the rainbow is true! The treasure is me and the treasure is you!

When you see these colours, remember what they said. When you are feeling sad say them out loud, or at least in your head.

Never forget you are beautiful and kind. You are smart, you are loved, and you have a great mind.